Home in Heaven

Hello, my name is Emma. I'm moving and it's really annoying. Dad says it's a must, but why can't we just stay here? I have to carry boxes and pack everything, even though I don't want to! Mom says I just have to accept it and stop complaining.

But I don't want to go away. Besides, my best friend Greta lives next door. How can I play with her in the future if I live so far away? My three teddies don't want to go in the boxes either. I'm sure they will be uncomfortable in the boxes because they are scared of the dark.

I don't think mom and dad really want to leave either. They seem very tense and sometimes the mood is really bad. They argue again about the smallest things, but I am sure it's because they are really sad.

Then why are they wanting to move? I don't understand! None of us want to leave and yet we still have to go! I even saw Mom crying. Dad only said, "We have to say goodbye to everything," and that was it.

I would much rather be with my grandma Anna now, because she is my favourite grandma. Whenever I am with her, she cooks my favourite food, spaghetti with tomato sauce. But now she is in hospital. I wonder if she gets that in the hospital too?

Hopefully she will get well soon, but mum always looks so weird when I ask her about it and then she cries. Dad only says that Grandma has a serious condition.

Why is Grandma in such a terrible state? I don't really know. She was once short like me, and had the same curly hair. Except hers was brown. Now her hair is grey and Granny is sick. She grew up on a farm with cows and horses, and in summer she used to eat fresh strawberries straight from the field. Grandma Anna even had her own dog named Charley and they were inseparable friends. He and Grandma both grew up together and then Grandma went to school - just like I soon will.

Later she drove a motorcycle without a license, was in gymnastics and had many friends.

Unfortunately Charley died sometime, because dogs do not live as long as we humans. Grandma was then very sad and missed him for a long long time. She cried a lot.

But then Grandpa came into her life. She started to see him more often and, in time, she also started to love him.

Then one summer evening she also met Jesus. But I never really understood that, because he wasn't there like Grandpa was. Did she love him too? And how can you love someone you can't see? But Jesus gave her a lot of strength, and Grandma even said that accepting Jesus was the best decision of her life.

From then on she mentioned Jesus a lot, and even talked to him. She called that praying and she often did it in the church service. But she said she could really talk to Jesus everywhere, and she did. Just imagine: Even though you can't see him, Jesus answers! No matter what question or concern Grandma Anna had, Jesus always listened to her. The answer from Jesus usually came in her mind.

When my mum and her two brothers were born, there was a lot happening! Grandma and Grandpa built a house, too. It was quite exhausting to do this while also bringing up three kids.

But those times were kind of great, too. Mom said she played and laughed a lot Besides, the house was really nice after it was finally finished. Grandma was young and fit then, too.

Unfortunately, today is different. A few hours ago mum got a phone call, and then she just cried. All of a sudden Dad was pale in the face, too. Then they called me to get ready, and we drove off in the car. When I asked where we were going, mom just started crying. After a few minutes we arrived at the hospital. Daddy said to me, "Your Grandma is dying, Sweetheart."

Everyone was crying, so dying must be something really bad. So I cried too. After all, I love Grandma. Who is going to cook the spaghetti when Grandma is busy dying? I hardly recognized her when we arrived in her room. She looked so thin and frail. We all told Grandma how much we love her and then she just closed her eyes. Her body was still there, but somehow Grandma was gone.

But, I really wanted to know where Granny is now. So I asked Mom about it. She just said, "Grandma is with Jesus now." But I didn't understand that, so I asked her again where Granny was. Mom just cried.

Now Dad stepped in and he began to explain: "Emma, your Grandma Anna is now in Heaven. "I said, "What is Heaven?" Papa smiled and asked, "What is the most beautiful place you can imagine?" "That's easy," replied Emma. "Last summer, when we jumped into the waves by the sea. No, even better were the mountains in winter and the snowball fight we had there."Dad laughed. "Yes, those were beautiful, but Jesus made the whole world with oceans and mountains and all the animals. And, he also made heaven, and heaven is a hundred times, probably a thousand times more beautiful. There's everything we humans could ever want in abundance!" I nodded my head, but somehow I didn't quite know what he meant by that.

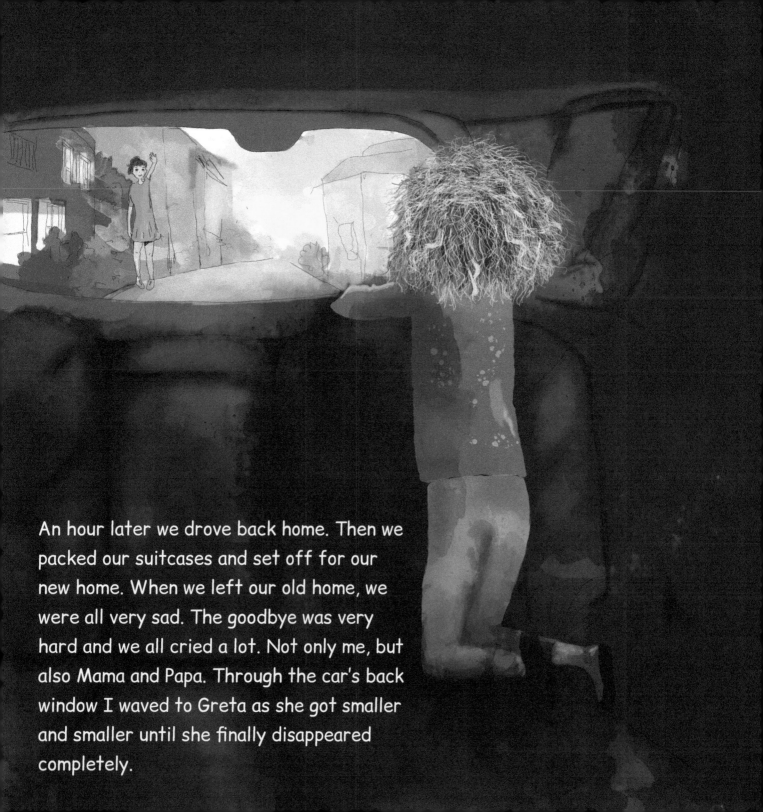

An hour later we drove back home. Then we packed our suitcases and set off for our new home. When we left our old home, we were all very sad. The goodbye was very hard and we all cried a lot. Not only me, but also Mama and Papa. Through the car's back window I waved to Greta as she got smaller and smaller until she finally disappeared completely.

A few days later Granny was buried, or rather what was left of her was. She didn't look like she used to. Somehow her body seemed empty, as though she had moved out. She was obviously now with Jesus. Then we said goodbye to Grandma, and my sad Grandpa who was also crying.

But one thing I was still unsure of: So I asked exactly that, "Why is everyone crying when Grandma's in heaven?" My parents replied tenderly:"We are so sad because we can't see her for a long time. It's a sort of temporary farewell, my darling."

I asked, "Can't Grandma just come back, you know, for a visit?" But Mum just said, "Sorry, darling, but one day, when you go to heaven, you'll see her again." Dying's a bit tricky, I guess. Maybe Grandma will make spaghetti up there again. And Daddy said Grandma wouldn't want to come back, because she's much better off in heaven with Jesus than she is here feeling sick.

When I arrived at our new house with mum and dad, I was amazed. It was really beautiful. The color, the windows and it even had a garden with butterflies and sunflowers. I immediately fell around my mum and dad's neck and screamed with joy. Then I saw another girl standing by the garden fence who wanted to play with me. She had funny red hair and she looked super nice. Her name was Amy and I'm sure her and I would become good friends. When I came home from playing in the evening, suddenly a clear idea came to my mind. "Mom! Dad! I think I understand," I shouted and then I told them. "Just like I moved out of my old house, Grandma moved out of her body. "The body was a bit old too, but now Grandma Anna is with Jesus.I bet he has a great new home for her too, and a new body too.So grandma can finally do her gymnastics again, and be with her dog Charley.

I am looking forward to see grandma again, and Jesus, but before I do I will play with Amy. In the next holidays I will visit Greta, jump into the sea, and have a snowball fight with dad. Every move hurts, but afterwards it gets better. Especially if you know Jesus.

Author: Stefan Waidelich

Illustration: Ana Rodić

ISBN: 9798687794473

1. Edition October 2020

© 2020 Stefan Waidelich Zeisigweg 6.72213 Altensteig

Print shop: Amazon Media EU S.á r.l., 5 Rue Plaetis, L-2338, Luxembourg

cover: Illustration Ana Rodić © Stefan Waidelich

Lightning Source UK Ltd.
Milton Keynes UK
UKHW050813090223
416624UK00003B/164